Creating Growth Focused Classrooms

Reflections and Strategies from a Teacher

Dr. Michelle Ihrig

Creating Growth Focused Classrooms: Reflections and Strategies from a Teacher
© 2022 by Dr. Michelle Ihrig. All Rights Reserved.

All rights reserved. No part of this book may be reproduced in any form or by any electronic or mechanical means, including information storage and retrieval systems, without permission in writing from the author. The only exception is by a reviewer, who may quote short excerpts in a review.

Cover designed by Dr. Michelle Ihrig

Live Growth Focused
www.LiveGrowthFocused.com

Printed in the United States of America

First Printing: July 2022
Live Growth Focused™

ISBN-13 978-1-946568-55-7

I dedicate this book to the
thousands of students
who shaped me into the educator
I am today, and to the
administrators and supervisors
who gave me the freedom to create,
to dream, and to inspire.

CONTENTS

Introduction	1
1. Mindset Matters	8
2. Philosophy Changes	16
3. Testing Temptations	32
4. The Logistics	42
5. Growth Activities	57
6. Communication	87
7. The Extras	104
8. Take Action	114
Action Plans	116
Notes and Doodles	121
About the Author	127

Introduction

Hello, Educator! I like to start my books with a letter to the reader. This book is a collection of reflections and strategies that are helpful to me in developing a growth mindset in my students. As you read this book, I hope you will find a few methods to adapt and add to your classroom to help your students grow.

Building relationships and goal-setting were already cornerstones of my teaching philosophy. However, I was first introduced to the concept of a growth mindset in 2016 when I listened to Dr. Carol Dweck's book *Mindset: The New Psychology of Success* just before the start of the school year. I was an Algebra 1 teacher at one of the largest high schools in my state. I had one class of students in which half were learning English, and the other half were juniors and seniors taking Algebra 1 for the 2nd or 3rd time. One of my classes was predominantly students with disabilities, one class was on-level students, and the final two classes were honors students. I share this because I want to show you that the concept of a growth mindset can work across levels, languages, and abilities.

Based on listening to Dweck's *Mindset*, I decided our class would focus on growth mindset and math. Our theme was Nosotros Crecemos en Matematicas: We Grow in Math. I spoke to my students about learning styles, goal setting, testing, grading, and my famous Planet Fitness story.

When it was time to take the PSAT, we set goals, and the students performed better than they expected. When it was time to take the mid-year STAR testing, my students again set goals, and their success was remarkable. Here are the highlights – and if you are a data person like me – the full results are on my website.

Of the 120 students I taught, 71 students demonstrated growth, and 47 students met their personal goals after just one semester. Ten students in my ELL/Repeater class moved up to the next level of mastery, while eight students in my PreAlgebra class moved. In my college prep class, there was not as much change; however, ten students met their personal goals. In my honors classes, where I initially questioned if teaching about growth mindset was worth our time, 13 students moved up a mastery level...again within one semester.

I wish I could take credit for being this awesome curriculum/content person. I am not that. I cannot tell you how one topic in Algebra 1 relates to PreCalc or another class. Manipulatives and project-based learning are not my favorites (though they have their places).

I am exceptional at motivating students to excel in life by developing a growth mindset. But, do my strategies work for every student all the time? No, some stragglers don't catch on by the end of the year and do not pass; however, my students' pass rate and standardized test scores tend to be consistently higher than their peers in other classes. The year my students encouraged me to write my first book about growth mindset, I was the highest performing teacher in my school and in the top 10% of the 12,000 teachers in my school district.

In my experience, I can tell you that for more students than I ever thought, investing the time to inspire students to excel in life by developing a growth mindset will make a difference in your classroom, your gradebook, and their lives.

You are probably somewhere on the spectrum between feeling energized to motivate students and feeling a bit awkward on the topic. Wherever you are and whatever your skill set, I suspect you could teach me many things I don't already know. Regardless of your current motivation or situation, I hope you find a few takeaways that will make your life easier and your students' futures brighter.

I designed this book to be a quick read (or skim). I used bold print to help you find the sections most relevant to you. Notes and Doodle pages follow each chapter for those who like to jot or draw a few things. There is some research, though not much. I hate reading about educational studies in professional development books. I prefer practical over scholarly in most situations because it is faster to adapt and implement. If an idea doesn't work for you, adjust it until it does or drop the concept entirely.

I close by sharing one more anecdote from that first growth-focused year. At the end of the semester, I asked students to reflect on how developing a growth mindset impacted them. I expected to read how they performed better in math, on the PSAT, or studied more; however, very few of their reflections included anything about math class.

Instead, I read how one student stopped getting involved with "girl drama" at school, how another student made the swim team, how a female student changed her relationship with her parents, and how several students decreased their use of technology. One of my favorite reflections was from a student who decided to have a growth mindset to improve his health. In one semester, he lost over 20 pounds and started to develop a six-pack. Who would have thought "We Grow in Math" would have stretched into so many facets of their lives.

My students taught me more about using a growth mindset than I did them. However, the influence of that first group of students led me to be even more deliberate in introducing the concept. This book is my effort to be a good steward of my students' collective wisdom over the years as I empower you to inspire your learners.

    We got this together!

Growth Mindset

The growth mindset impacted my math grade in a big way. Growth mindset encouraged me to put in more effort in this class. Consequently my tests grades started to go up. Overall growth mindset made me a better person. I say this because before growth mindset I would complain and come up with excuses for my failures. After growth mindset I stopped complaining and started to make excuses to win.

Love this!

Woohoo!

Growth mindset has also helped me in many other things in my life. For example going into my 9th grade year I would make excuses about how I didn't have a good 8th grade football season. After growth mindset I started working and started varsity as a freshman.

This is fantastic! Way to go!

Notes and Doodles

Dr. Michelle Ihrig

Chapter 1
Mindset Matters

Take a moment to reflect on one of your "high-flyers." Now, I am not speaking about the gifted or accelerated students who will do anything you ask of them. Instead, picture the student who struggles to sit, may talk out of turn, or might be a hall-wanderer. Perhaps, it is the student who will cause you to let out a slight sigh of relief if they are absent. Perhaps such a student never graced your classroom, or you don't want to admit you ever felt this way, which is okay.

For over 20 years, I worked with thousands of students. Every year, I have someone who is this person for me – at least in the beginning. But, by the end of the year, I see the student differently, and we both grow through the process. The point is, it is okay to admit that there is (at least) one student who may be a struggle. However, it is also equally essential to ensure you give this student every opportunity to succeed. When we look at our students as young people with dreams and obstacles, we stop being teachers of content and start being teachers of the future.

In my first years of teaching, I learned almost every behavior we see is impacted by some previous situation or circumstance. Allow me to reminisce about my first two years as a teacher. I was 21 years old, and several of my students turned 19 while I taught them. We were a small class of 20 students, and many participated in a vocational program part of the day.

Because I was young, I made some mistakes. For example, I was not too fond of our room; it was so gloomy and bland. So, one day I stayed late and sponge-painted the large wall (without permission). Kids can't learn when they're hungry, so I always had milk, bread, peanut butter, and jelly for students to make whenever they were hungry. (This was in 2000 before peanut allergies flooded schools.)

I remember one student who was a thorn in my side. He had been sent out of other classrooms and ended up with me. Somehow, he found time to get stoned between his vocational classes and my program almost daily. He was at least two state tests away from graduating, spoke like a sailor, and smelled like one, too (no offense to sailors).

I will never forget the day he told me he enlisted in the Navy. I didn't believe him and thought he was pulling my leg. Lo and behold, a week later, in Spring 2001, I received a call from Officer Isler, who asked how the student was doing. I was stunned. I realized my student might not make it unless I changed my mindset about his future. My mindset about his future was equally or even more critical than his mindset of himself.

Through hard work and focus, he passed his state tests and graduated. Three months later, he reported to Boot Camp a few weeks after September 11th, 2001. Just before that Christmas, the student, who one year prior sat in our comfy orange chairs wearing a red hoodie and black winter hat while stoned out of his mind, stood before me in his Navy uniform. Mindset matters.

During my second year of teaching, one of my students cursed even more than the previously discussed student. But, the thing that was so annoying was that it was without meaning. "Anyone see my f—ing pencil? Could you please help me with this f—ing assignment?" Yes, please, and the f-word in the same request! But, because there was no ill-will, and there was usually remorse, I decided to work with the student instead of writing referral after referral (more on that in Chapter 7).

After a few weeks, though, I hit my limit. So, I called home. Dad's greeting: "Hi, how's your f—ing day going?" Dad didn't even realize he was swearing. Curse words were part of the everyday conversation at home. Eventually, the student and I made it through. We still had our moments, though. He was the student who thought it might be a good idea to discretely add dish soap to my bubble tube by the window. The result? A volcanic eruption of suds covered everything on the counter. My response? Pure laughter. Mindset matters.

Haim G. Ginott was an Israel-born educator who graduated from Columbia University's Teacher College in 1948 and eventually earned his doctorate in clinical psychology from Columbia University in 1952.

In his 1972 book, *Teacher and Child*, Dr. Ginott shared the following reflection that he penned as a young teacher:

> I have come to a frightening conclusion.
> I am the decisive element in the classroom.
> It is my personal approach that creates the climate.
> It is my daily mood that makes the weather.
> As a teacher I possess the tremendous power
> to make a child's life miserable or joyous.
> I can be a tool of torture
> or an instrument of inspiration.
> I can humiliate or humor, hurt or heal.
> In all situations it is my response that decides
> whether a crisis will be escalated or de-escalated
> and a student humanized or de-humanized.

Time for the tricky question: has there ever been a time when you (intentionally or not) brought more gloom than sunshine? It happens. This book will help you to create a plan so it doesn't happen again (Chapter 8).

Developing a Growth Mindset in Teaching

I would like you to think of a time when you felt proud of something you did. It can be minor, like finishing a workout, getting your grades in early, or creating a new recipe. Recently, I developed a go-to healthy salad and, in excitement, called my mom to share the recipe. Even small moments of success can elicit a great sense of pride.

Perhaps your proud moment might be much larger, like finishing a college course for your Specialist's degree, watching your child walk across the graduation stage, or some other monumental moment.

Now, pause and soak in the memory. Think about how you felt, why you felt that way, and how long the feeling lasted.

Seriously, pause and enjoy the moment.

How did the memory make you feel? Did you feel like you could do anything? Did you feel accomplished? Did you feel like the world was your oyster?

This feeling is precisely what growth-focused teachers want their students to feel daily. You may think helping students to be proud of their accomplishments is exhausting to do...and in the beginning, it is VERY exhausting. I don't want to paint pictures of unicorns and rainbows and tell you it is easy. It can be; however, working with our "high-flyers" can be tiresome, discouraging, but worth it.

A growth-focused teacher helps students to celebrate genuine, little successes. These small successes will evolve into more considerable achievements and, eventually, a behavior change for you and your students.

Throughout this book, I will share with you the strategies I found successful in changing my mindset (first) and then my students' mindsets. I'll discuss my philosophy about grades and testing, setting up the physical space, what to cover the first week, activities, communication, and a few extras. Take what is helpful to you, adapt what could be useful, and leave the rest. This process involves discovering what is best for you and your teaching style.

Just remember, very few, if any, students wake up thinking, "I want today to be a tough day for me. I want to perform poorly on a test, or I can't wait to feel discouraged." Similarly, I doubt any of us wake up thinking, "I can't wait to make my students' days miserable."

We all want "good days." We all want to leave school feeling accomplished and proud. The difference between you and your students is the power for a good day to happen lies almost entirely in your hands.

> I feel that the growth mindset is useful in math. I think so because with a growth mindset, I can be successful in math. For example, if I were to get a failing grade on a pretest, a growth mindset will help me get a passing grade on the unit test. I think that having a growth mindset will help me in all areas of my life, including school. A growth mindset will help me create a sense of positivity and motivation within myself. Although I don't have a complete growth mindset, I'm working on myself and trying to find ways to better myself. I have a growth mindset on growth mindset.
>
> ↑ *love this line!*

Notes and Doodles

Chapter 2
Philosophy Changes

A growth-focused teacher focuses on the process, not the result. I realize this may be counter-intuitive because a growth-focused teacher also helps students set goals with the intent of achieving the goals; however, the process remains more important than the result.

Before I jump into how I set up my physical or virtual classrooms and the activities my students complete, I decided it was more important to jump ahead and talk about my philosophy regarding grades and assessment. This order should make sense to many of you. We "start with the end in mind" when we write curriculum or lessons. First, we consider the standards, the depths of knowledge we want our students to reach, and the assessments they will take. Then we work backward to form the lessons. For those interested, Grant Wiggins and Jay McTighe first introduced the concept of backward design in *Understanding by Design* (1998).

I believe it is essential to talk about grades and assessments first because if we don't, the setup of the classroom and the activity recommendations will make little sense. Remember, this book is all about the *process* of creating growth-focused classrooms.

Process Over Result

A growth-focused teacher cares about the process more than the result. Why? Because process leads to growth.

Think about your actual "high-flyer" student, not the learner from the previous chapter. Instead, it is the accelerated student who can listen (or even half-listen) to your lesson once and can complete most of the problems. Perhaps the elementary student who wrote an entire story while you were still teaching how to write a topic sentence.

True "high-flyers" will be successful, in traditional ways, with little intervention. Are they excited about learning? Sometimes. Are they motivated to push themselves farther? Possibly, but only when challenged. Still, because they earn the coveted A, they may not be the focus of our attention during the school day.

What happens to these students when they experience a challenge? Will they persevere? Possibly. If they don't reach success, will they keep striving? Not likely. In Dweck's TedTalk, *The Power of Yet*, available on YouTube, she describes what happens to students who focus on grades instead of the process. In one study, students admitted to the desire to cheat rather than study for the next test. In another study, students said they would look for someone who did worse than them to feel better. Neither one of these thoughts are positive.

Instead, we must teach all students to focus on the process. I tell my students that their brains should hurt every day because they are thinking. For my true "high-flyers," this may mean providing accelerated work at higher DOK levels. For my on-level students, it may also mean providing accelerated work.

I am a lesson planner. When I taught in person, I would plan my entire unit and make the copies weeks before the unit started. My packets were massive – 20 pages each (10 double-sided). Within the packet would be everything my students needed about the unit, with a focus on differentiation. Every student had access to accelerated activities, on-level activities, and remediation. Did I spend hours putting it together? Yes. Did I need to lesson plan any other time during the unit? Nope. It was already done.

Now that I teach online, I do the same thing. I construct units at a time. I teach an advanced class; however, all my students get access to the advanced curriculum to develop a deeper understanding of the content.

Webb's Depth of Knowledge (DOK)

In 1997, Norman Webb from the Wisconsin Center for Education Research released Webb's Depth of Knowledge, a way to categorize activities of thinking. Here is a brief overview for those who might be new to the concept.

Level 1 – Recall

Sample Problem: 3+2=

Why: Students simply need to use the standard algorithm to answer the question.

Level 2 – Skill/Concept

Sample Problem: In a duck pond, there were 12 ducks. Three ducks flew away. Two ducks walked away. How many ducks left the pond?

Why: First, some extra information is shared. "There were 12 ducks." Students need to decide how to address the additional information. Next, the problem includes the numbers two and three, yet the operation is not provided; students must determine whether to add or subtract. Third, the word "left" implies subtraction; however, the problem is solved using addition. In conclusion, students need to understand the concepts of addition and subtraction to know how to solve this problem.

Level 3 – Strategic Thinking

Sample Problem: In a duck pond, there were 12 ducks. Some of them left. How many? Where did they go? Write number sentences to demonstrate what happened.

Why: First, there is no one correct answer. Did one duck leave or seven? Certainly, 3.4 ducks didn't leave; why? Next, the problem integrates math with a constructed response. Students need to decide what happened and then explain their thinking. Did the ducks fly, waddle, or dance away? Lastly, students need to provide mathematical reasoning to explain what happened.

Level 4 – Extended Thinking

Sample Problem: The Old MacDonald Farm wants to protect the duck pond from predators. What are some natural predators to ducks? Are there other predators? What could the MacDonald's do to reduce the impact of predators? Which solution is the best?

Why: Level 4 is all about extended thinking. Students will need time to research the topic. Learners should evaluate and make decisions about the options. Level 4 tasks require longer than a single class period. They are also not simply extended projects, like a poster project that takes three days. There needs to be a deeper understanding of the content and critical thinking about the concept.

Growth-Focused Grading

Disclaimer: This section is how I grade my students and the opportunities I provide them. It will be necessary that you loop in your administrative team and your content team. If there is opposition, that's okay. Good dialogue helps all of us grow. You may need to wait on some ideas for a while; however, you can implement many of these strategies without giving your group an unfair advantage over others. Transparently, I feel this way of working is more challenging for students than the policies of some of my colleagues over the years.

Earning an A is both accessible and challenging in my class. My students are graded based on mastery of content. A portion of the grade (40%) is from completing formative assessments, which help students move through the curriculum. All students should be able to earn A's on the formative assessments. Summative assessments comprise 60% of the overall grade, and my summative assessments are not easy A's on the first attempt.

I focus on a version of standards-based grading. Looking at my gradebook, you will see the specific concepts I expect my students to learn. The grade they receive reflects their mastery of that content.

My students rarely complete a DOK 1 assignment and earn a grade because DOK 1 questions are not good indicators of mastery. The classwork, formative, and summative assessments nearly always include at a minimum DOK 1 and DOK 2 problems. Almost always, I grade for accuracy, not completion. If students are learning a new topic and have formative work to complete that evening, they may score low because they are still at a DOK 1 level with the content...and I still put the grade in the gradebook.

It is entirely possible for a student to complete every assignment and still fail the course. For some people reading this line may be a challenge. Families understandably struggle when their child first comes to my class. Because if a student knows only 50% of the content but completed 100% of the formative assignment, the grade entered is 50%, representing their mastery level. Chapter 6 includes more information about the specifics of my grades and how I communicate with families about current levels of mastery.

We live in a world where completion is acceptable. We drive to work each day, and unless we open a safe-driving app on our phone, we are not graded by how much over the speed limit we went, how many yellow lights we accelerated through, or how many people were not so happy to see us driving. We got to our destination...the result, not the process, mattered.

A football team might have the better defensive line, but the opposing team may have a slightly better offense. Who is recognized? The team with the higher score at the end of the game. The win mattered more than the number of sacks the defense completed compared to the other team.

So for many families, seeing their students with failing grades can be frustrating until I explain my grading philosophy, where we celebrate growth and mastery over completion. Then they understand.

First, students can redo any assignment until the last few days of the marking period. Yes, EVERY assignment, EVERY student. So regardless if it was late, messy, or missing the first time, there is always an opportunity to do it again, even a third time. Why? Because process (and mastery) matters.

Didn't score well the first time? Great, try again. Still don't get it? That's okay. Did you find another resource to help? Did you connect with the free virtual tutors paid for by the district? Nope, okay. Let me show you how to access that support first, and then if the topic is still a struggle, I will help you out.

Why do I expect students to look for other resources or contact the virtual tutor instead of coming to me first? Because I will not be with them after they leave my class. It is more important that my students learn how to help themselves and persevere first; the intellectual struggle is a positive feeling.

I realize some elementary teachers might question my belief in enabling students to find their answers independently. Here's the thing: When a child wants to learn how to play an online game, do you or their parents teach them how to play it? I doubt it. The child likely searched for how to play the game on YouTube, was likely successful, and started playing. Let's help our learners transfer the ability to search for information to academics, like when they need to structure an essay, complete a math problem, or learn about electricity.

We must encourage our students to be independent and know when they need help. Spending a few weeks or months helping them help themselves will change the course of your classroom and instruction. Your students will truly learn to be growth-focused.

Further, when you equip students with the skills to get help (not answers) through investigations, you may find that their first-attempt formative scores will start to increase. Instead of just guessing for completion, when they are working on their assignments at home, many of your learners will take the time to look up help first so they won't have to do the task again later.

Benefits of Virtual Instruction

I love teaching online. Not only am I part of a fantastic staff, but teaching, grading, and providing feedback are much more manageable. There are no packets to copy. Students receive instant feedback, and flipped classroom models can yield more time for targeted small groups. In addition, there are more accessible opportunities for differentiation. If I ever return to in-person teaching again, I will keep this model for formative assessments.

A slight disclaimer: what follows are my favorite tools for formative assessments. There are many, many others that my colleagues at my school prefer over what I use. That's why we are teachers and not tutors! Our responsibility is to do the best for our students using our teaching styles. So you do what's best for you and take what I share next with perhaps a more prominent grain of salt than other concepts in the book.

EdPuzzle: I love this platform. Every topic I cover with my students includes an accompanying EdPuzzle… some that I made and many that I adapted. As a word of caution: If you are a 1:1 district and your district banned YouTube, you will need to search for EdPuzzle-hosted videos so your students can use the technology without issue.

Why does EdPuzzle work for me? First, students can see another person teaching the content. Have you ever taught a topic for two days, then one of your other students rephrases what you said, and suddenly the confusion other students were experiencing dissipated? Simply having another voice share the same information differently can help.

Next, EdPuzzle allows for embedded questions. The video will cease moving forward until the learner answers the question. If they are stuck, the student can re-watch that part of the video clip. Plus, the creativity and visuals are better than I can produce in my available time. I might use someone else's video and embed my DOK 1 and DOK 2 questions.

Lastly, it is super-easy to reset a student's progress. Once I type the grade into my gradebook, I typically will reset any assignments less than 80% for the student to try again. Giving them an instant second attempt works SO well. The students get second access to the content without me needing to sit next to them. They can continue to work through mastery outside of the school day and still be successful.

<u>Classkick:</u> Another favorite resource you should ask your school to invest in is the Pro Version of Classkick. All the worksheets I used to give in packets are now uploaded

as PDFs digitally. Further, I embed answer boxes into each question I want my students to complete. If it is a simple response, like a number or a word, the program will grade the answer and provide the student instant feedback - a must-have in math.

Students can write or type in the platform or write on paper and then upload their work. Teachers can grade essays simply and provide immediate feedback to students in real-time.

The teacher dashboard is incredible. I can view the top third of all my students' work simultaneously with a simple scroll. Also, a hand-raise feature allows me to help students at the moment. Finally, using the chat feature, I can leave notes on the side of the assignment and track how much support I provided.

Flipgrid: Flipgrid is free and allows for DOK 2 and some DOK 3 level work. My content team decided that students would record a presentation about one skill they learned for each unit. Our expectations are high. We share the best videos with our classes as another tool for mastering content.

In closing, switching how you consider grades could make one of the most significant impacts on your learners. Because of the inclusion of DOK 2 content on day one of a topic, your actual "high flyers" will learn the value of learning as a process. Your struggling students will know that they can retry any assignment. The F is not failure. It simply instructs the teacher and student on the present mastery level and what is "not yet" mastered.

Further, if it were not for the inclusion of the technology tools listed above, I would probably go insane with all the grading and regrading. I used EdPuzzle, Classkick, and Flipgrid before I switched to online teaching. If you are a teacher, especially at a 1:1 school, talk with your admin about including the Pro versions if your district does not already have similar products. Depending on the size of your school, the investment could be $2,000-$5,000 for the software above. The savings from paper, toner, and wear-and-tear on the copiers could help offset the costs. However, the most critical value will be the increased access and immediate feedback your students will have with the lessons you present.

Growth mindset is what helped helped impact my grade. Growth mindset changed me forreal. What I mean by this is that, I stopped making excuses. And went myself "lemme just do it now" cus i wouldnt want to do it later. Its the fact that i always tell my sister to "be compient" and "have a growth mindset" because Mr. robinson says "be compient" and you say "growth mindset." These days i guess its all about growth mindset. Ever since i learned about it, i wanted to do better

Growth Mindset!

Gwen – Thank you for sharing! Well Done! – Dr. Ihrig

excellent intro!

I think that Growth Mindset impacts my scores in math because they help you believe that there's still hope to get higher grades even if you haven't done good in the past. I recieved 5% on my Unit 2 pretest. But yesterday I recieved a 77%. Although I wasn't happy with my grade I could see a little improvement. I want MUCH BETTER grades in the future. Because I'm such a perfectionist it's easier for me to get dissappointed & feel like I failed. Although it's hard for me to think that there's hope. In all honesty having a Growth Mindset requires patience. Patience isn't my best trait LOL! *mine either!* But I plan on trying my best, studying, and finding new resources/roundines that help me understand the material better. I think that Growth Mindset is great but there comes a time where the fact of the matter is that you failed or you did bad. Sometimes I get annoyed because when I fail a test and you say I can do better next time, although that's true the negativity still affects my grade & it also makes me feel like I don't get the material & it's not like I can redo it or anything. It's going to take a while but I'm going to put Growth Mindset on my Geometry grade & other areas of my grade.

– Growth Mindset also affect my Biology grade because I was doing bad but now she's gone.

we all get the perfectionist thoughts sometimes.

When it comes to grades– that is true.

you can improve on the final though!

Notes and Doodles

Chapter 3
Testing Temptations

Testing is one of those topics which can be the ultimate stressor for students, teachers, and families. Unfortunately, there are so many different schools of thought. I once worked with an administrator who felt that all formalized testing should be eliminated and students should only develop in their abilities. While I fully respect that administrator and those who think similarly, I disagree.

There are gaps in our students' performance, and the 2020 pandemic extended those gaps even more. To only test based on a child's ability and remove standardized testing at local and state levels deny educators the ability to consistently determine areas of strengths and areas that require further exploration and remediation.

I do believe that tests need to be meaningful. I've worked in districts where teachers made their tests, and I've taught in districts that provided the same test for all 6,000 students in the content area. Allowing individual teachers, or even individual content teams, to devise their own tests can cause inconsistent performance and mastery across classrooms and schools.

My students know that my favorite days are "test-taking days," and by the end of the first semester, they are also their favorite days. Why? Because every test is meaningful.

First, I strive to give my students pre-tests before we even begin learning the concept. Then, as a class, we look at our results, and individually, students will see which standards they need to focus on the most. We also set goals for what they want to achieve on their practice test.

The practice test? Yes, my students will take at least two tests at the end of each unit. The first test (called the practice test) is one that I create, and the second test, taken at the same time as their peers in other classes, is the content-team approved test. Note: I share my first test and the accompanying resources with my colleagues if they want to implement it. How are the tests meaningful? Because we use the results of the first test to inform the areas that need further study before the next test.

Yes, WE use the results. I teach my students to be data analysts. The score on the practice test becomes the test grade in the gradebook. My students view the test questions they missed and are required to review and study them to deepen their understanding.

How do my students review? Well, I upload the practice test to Classkick. The document includes a blank test for them to look at independently, videos I created on completing each question, and my full answer key. The next day, I might explain any questions my students still had, and then they take the content team test the next day. If the second test grade is higher than the first, I will replace the score in the gradebook.

So why do I call the first test the "practice test" even though it is a real, graded test? I call it "practice" to decrease test anxiety and get an accurate read on my students' strengths and needs.

Further, my tests are almost always more challenging than my content team's. Why? Because I make them challenging on purpose. There is an even (or even skewed) distribution of DOK 2 questions compared to DOK 1. Why? Because the state tests will have DOK 2 questions. I believe we are doing a disservice to our students if we limit their exposure to these types of questions. Also, we strive for mastery, and higher DOKs demonstrate a deeper understanding of the concepts.

Why does the practice test grade go in the gradebook? Because I want my students to realize what their overall grades could be if they don't set goals, study, and strive for mastery. Also, it helps decrease test anxiety the second time because no matter their score on the second test, their overall grade can only go up.

Celebrations in Data

When I taught at the high school level, we would also have Data Days that we did after we took both unit tests. I would create elaborate slideshows which would reveal my students' collective scores based on who reached mastery and how the classes performed compared to their peers. Here is an example from one of the standards:

AKS	Description	PreTest	Ihrig	Growth	GCPS	District Diff	SGHS	SGHS Diff
MAGE.B.10 2Q	explain how the criteria for triangle congruence (ASA, SAS, and SSS) follow from the definition of congruence in terms of rigid motions	15.7%	54.5%	38.8%	42.9%	11.6%	41.5%	13.0%

Notice how I first listed the PreTest score on the standard, then our mean score, followed by the growth in our percentage. Then, we compared our score to the school and county's mean.

We would celebrate our data for EACH standard after every test, even when they performed lower than their peers. At the end of the semester, we also looked at our class progression for total mastery of the content.

	Test Average	Beginning	Developing	Proficient	Distinguished
Semester 1 Pretest	14.6%	100%	0%	0%	0%
Interim	47%	74.2%	15.7%	10.1%	0%
Final Raw	51.1%	61.8%	27%	11.2%	0%
Final Converted	71%	30.3%	13.5%	44.9%	11.2%

I cannot overstate the importance of reviewing data with your students routinely. It will drastically remove the sting of low grades while cementing the value of being growth-focused.

Testing Temptations to Overcome

The following are some of my testing temptations and those I witnessed from my colleagues over the years.

1) <u>Don't help.</u> In my early years and on classroom tests, there were a few occasions I gave my students (as a class) a hint to make it through a challenging problem. I justified my actions because I valued the grade over their growth. Please don't do this. Giving tips will invalidate your data.

2) <u>Easy tests.</u> Low DOK level tests are a calamity I used to fall into when I was all about drill and practice. When we give our students tests

predominantly at a Recall (DOK 1) level, we learn if they know the algorithm or can answer a simple question. We do not determine if they understand the topic well enough to apply their knowledge.

3) <u>Testing a concept only once.</u> I am usually a level-headed teacher until I feel like I am on a time constraint. It can be tempting to remove the first test and not offer remediation because of time. I would use the excuse that only half of my students understood the topic, so I needed the extra day to review the topic with everyone. NO! Please don't do that. Use your time and your tests wisely. Once the students complete the practice test, share with the students the items they missed, and then let each student spend the day going through the content they individually need.

4) <u>Calling all long projects tests.</u> I know some admin and I will likely differ on this topic, and it's okay. Let me make my case. How many teachers expect students to recreate the solar system or a similar DOK 1 project? I am not sure, but the project takes hours of class time and home time. Why is the project relevant or meaningful? What is it evaluating? Students can easily use Google to learn anything they need to know about the

qualities of the solar system. What deeper thinking happened about the topic? Okay, you might think I will add a higher-level aspect to make the project meaningful because I love seeing what they create. So, you are adding more time to the project to justify seeing their creativity? Why not just provide them with a higher-level project?

Here is an example of a project you could ask your students to complete that would be meaningful, align with the standards, and hopefully fun. You and your friends decide to open a fitness center on [planet]. What are some of the obstacles you will face? How could you overcome the challenges? How will gravity impact the fitness center? What new exercises could you offer based on the planet's qualities? What assumptions do you need to make about operating a fitness center on [planet]? After each student or group creates their display, host a gallery walk. Then assign a follow-up task: What did you learn about each planet? What planet would you want to exercise on and why?

Do you notice how this is still a project about the solar system; however, it is no longer a DOK

1 level project. Instead, it is a high DOK 3 and possibly a DOK 4 and still exciting for the students and fun for you.

5) <u>Skipping the goal setting.</u> Most of us have participated in at least one training about creating SMART goals (Specific, Measurable, Attainable, Realistic, and Time-Bound). Nearly every December 30th, there will be some news story about being specific about New Year's resolutions. So, if we are to be SMART about our goals, why not help our students be SMART in creating theirs? It does not need to be very involved. Perhaps at the start of the test, you ask students to write what score they think they will earn. We do not want 100s on every paper because it is not realistic. After they take the first test, the students reflect on what they earned and now set a goal to work toward for the second test based on how much effort they are willing to commit to studying. These few extra minutes will make a difference in their outlook on learning.

You are in control of your classroom. Remember, this book is not about telling you what to do. Instead, it is about sharing my process for creating growth-focused classrooms. I hope you take just a few concepts to heart to start and then progress from there. No one has all the answers, not even me. The dynamics of our classes are different; our teaching style, content, and a thousand other things are different.

What needs to be the same is our willingness to see the value of creating an atmosphere for students to excel in life with a growth mindset.

Unit 2 pretest: 26%

Unit 2b test: 80%

On the pretest my score was 26%. The growth mindset improve my score alot. On the unit 2b test my score was 80%. My score jump 54%. I think growth mindset help my score alot, because I went from an F to a B on the test. Actually beside growth mindset help me improve my score Dr. Ihrig were also the one that alway cheer up me and made me feel comfortable on learning.

Notes and Doodles

Chapter 4
The Logistics

Once we adopt the mindset of being a growth-focused educator, we must change the classroom environment to be the same. This chapter is a collection of suggestions for your physical or virtual classrooms. So, take what you love, adapt what you like, and leave the rest.

Bulletin Boards I love posters – as long as they are meaningful. One year that I taught summer school, the teacher's room I used was beautiful, and the boards were well done – if you stood right next to the board to read the encouraging words. Unfortunately, a zoned-out student who needs a brain break cannot be inspired in 20-point font. Here is a picture from my classroom in the 2018-2019 school year:

Now, transparently, the immense Growth Focused sign was a bit of an overstatement. The poster was supposed to be smaller, and my friend in the print shop made it the wrong size. Yet, it was readable and meaningful.

The Proud 2B phrase is part of our PBIS motto; I simply added the descriptors underneath. Gritty and a Problem Solver were posters over the front board. Above the shelves, you can see Proud 2B a Problem Solver. Coincidently, the boxes you see on the shelves are my students' boxes which they used to store their unit packets. Giving a designated space prevented packets from being left at home, lost, or damaged.

Do my students seem focused on their computer screens? They should. It was test-taking day! The folders were the dividers for those sitting at the tables.

Now, the large sign stays the entire year, and the content around the poster will change. It is usually student work – not about math – but growth mindset. It might be reflections from people who allowed me to display their work, posters on SMART goals, or a big data display.

Do I need them to be able to read their peers' work when they need a brain break? No; however, when they see the growth-focused assignment on the board, it could trigger a reflection on their work from the assignment, which can be inspiring because it is meaningful to them.

In the virtual environment, we do not have ways to display student work so efficiently. So instead, I change my Zoom background daily. There are days that I will change the background multiple times during class. For example, if kids seem to be checking out, I might change my background to a screen of flying hotdogs.

When I am first introducing the concept or when students might need a bit of encouragement, I will change the background to something growth-focused, even if it is only for five minutes. The variety will make it interesting.

Flexible Seating Here comes another thing I love: flexible seating. If you look at the picture of my classroom, you can see that I brought in comfortable chairs and dining room tables, narrow conference tables, and a few single desks. Giving students assigned seats for the entire year, semester, or month can be tempting. I don't. Instead, I set very high expectations for the first month. Then once the students internalize my expectations, they have the freedom to sit where they please.

When do I use assigned seats after? For every test. This decreases the likelihood of cheating from a pre-arranged dialogue. There are also days when I have assignments that require particular grouping for differentiation, so the assigned seats will reappear then.

In a virtual environment, there are no seats. When we complete virtual group work, there may be some assignments where I let them pick their groups, others where I designate the groups, and still, others where I share my screen, and a digital team generator will set the groups for me.

Who Needs Help Table I am not sure about your class sizes; however, my classes are typically at or above capacity. Therefore, jumping over book bags to reach students is a nightmare. Also, generally, multiple students need help with the same content. My solution: the Who Needs Help Table.

After I teach the mini-lesson, I immediately go to the table to help anyone still stuck. The Who Needs Help Table is fantastic because those who did not need me to complete another whole-class problem could move on, and those who need help will get support.

My favorite table was a 4' Bistro table that I raised using pavers; it is labeled in the picture at the start of the chapter. A standing height eliminated the need for chairs as students could comfortably stand around the table to get help. I also had a mobile whiteboard that I could use to reteach any concept.

So, what about the student who didn't want to get help? Too bad I called them over anyway. There is little to no stigma from people who get help because the tone in the classroom is growth. Each student, especially the unmotivated, knows that process is more important than the grade. We celebrate 50% as much as we celebrate 90% because both grades demonstrate what areas the students mastered and which areas need a revisit.

In the virtual environment, I provide help in two ways. First, I do not believe students should be sitting and on camera every minute of the school day. So, once I presented the mini-lesson and answered any questions, I might dismiss specific students early to work independently. Now, I am available to support students who still need help without distracting others who don't.

For example, on Day 1 of the topic, once the students are logged into EdPuzzle and have the video ready to play, they type in the box that they are "good to go" and are dismissed. Because I put grades into the gradebook daily, which is so easy if you use EdPuzzle and Classkick, the students know if they do not complete the task, their grades will drop. Plus, watching a video and working on problems while the teacher is talking to other students is distracting.

If it is Day 2 of the task, we are likely working in Classkick. These days, students raise their hands in Classkick (not Zoom), which allows me to jump to their screen. Instead of talking, I can type feedback to them in their assignment chat. If I notice a consistent area of need, I might gain everyone's attention for a few moments to address the misconception.

Lighting Classrooms can be sterile. Therefore, I often bring in floor lamps, which is especially helpful in rooms with no windows and you need to keep some lights on for students to write notes while a video is playing. Also, I frequently use the floor lamps instead of the overall lamps right after lunch. It decreases the stimulation from the lunchroom and helps my students focus.

Further, I invest in fluorescent light shades that are made from fire-resistant fabric and attach with magnets to the overhead lights. I prefer the beige shades, though some of my colleagues prefer the blue-toned ones. Just ensure that whichever ones you purchase come with a safety certificate. Then take a picture of the certificate and email the picture to yourself with the subject "Fire Marshall" Then, keep the original safe. I guarantee you the Fire Marshall will ask for it during their visits.

In a virtual environment, I ensure students can see my face clearly. If too much light is behind me, I will look like a shadow, not a teacher. Plus, I use facial expressions when I teach, so a clear, lit face is imperative.

Mints I invest in mints and keep them easily accessible to students. A quick Google search will show you the benefits of peppermint and the brain. Does it make you smarter? Nope, but it does stimulate the Hippocampus area of the brain, which addresses mental clarity and memory. The smell will trigger the partaker's brain as well as those in the nearby vicinity.

When I started teaching, I purchased peppermint patties from the bulk food store, but they were expensive. So now I spend about $10 for 363 Lifesaver Mints. You might think the kids abuse it and fill in their pockets, but I haven't had an issue. I just set boundaries about the trash.

I do not have tips for mints in a virtual environment other than encouraging students to get up and get some water to drink. The movement from their computer screen to another space for water should be enough to refresh their brain and help them to refocus.

Quick Food Note You might have noticed in the picture at the start of the chapter the empty cereal container and a few food wrappers. I let my students eat during class, as long as the food doesn't end up on my floor and is not a distraction. Kids cannot learn effectively if they are hungry. Also, although I do not provide peanut butter and jelly, like in my first years of teaching, I keep stashes of fruit snacks (for those with allergies) as well as digestive crackers in my cabinet. Students have free access to get what they need, as long as they let me know first.

Are you running a program after school? Consider connecting with the head of your food service program. Some states allow the allocation of federal dollars to serve nutritious after-school snacks. For example, in the state of Georgia, it is called the At-Risk Afterschool Meals Program, a component of the Child and Adult Care Food Program. So the answer might be "no," and it could also be "yes."

Daily Agenda Posting the daily agenda on the board will help your students stay on task. In many elementary classrooms, the daily agenda might be the class schedule. My agenda is slightly different and follows this pattern:

Component	Reason
Date	Track work, know which notes they need if absent
Topic	Focus of the day, know which topic to search for if they need more help
Essential Questions/"I can"	Sets the goal for the day
Tasks	With time stamps and learning styles to help them stay focused and know what's coming
Homework	If there is any – usually just to finish the formative classwork
Upcoming Dates	Projected practice test and unit test dates

In a virtual environment, I use my Zoom background to post relevant information. First, I design the background in PowerPoint – then "Save As" the slide as a .png or export it as a movie.

The essential question is on the left and the agenda on the right. I will also post the image in my virtual classroom, and if I use folders or modules, I will upload the image there.

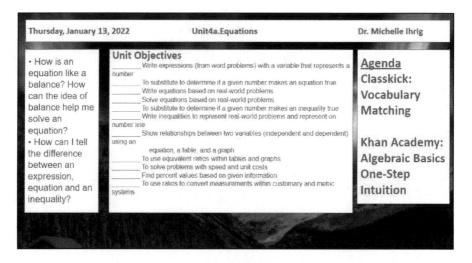

At the start of the unit, I will include the essential questions and schedule; however, I will also have the unit objectives. For the first five minutes of class, I will move from the camera, and we will go through the topics. I will also ask students if any topics are familiar to them. It may also be the day students will take the pre-test for the unit.

Below is an agenda for a lighter academic day. First, as it was right before Spring Break and a data day, we spent about five minutes learning about crayons. Then we reviewed our data, and students went to USA Test Prep to work on targeted objectives.

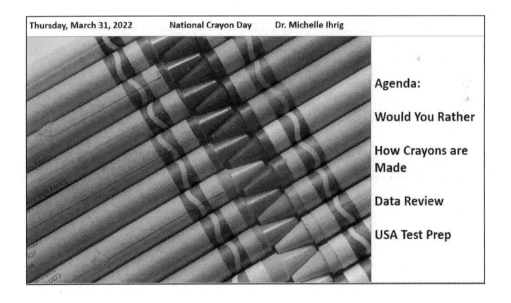

Brain Breaks Years ago, I heard that our attention spans are about one minute per year of age up until about 20 minutes. Then we will need a change in activities or a brain reset. For example, think about a professional development session you may have sat in where the presenter just spoke, especially after lunch. How long did it take you to start thinking about your grocery list, what you needed to do after the session or your plans for the weekend?

For this book, I tried to find the actual statistic. Instead, I read in multiple sources that we can expect children to pay attention for 2-3 minutes per year of age. While I still believe 20-25 minutes is a good time to do a brain reset, you will know based on the activity what your students need.

One of the strategies I teach my students and implement in the classroom is the Pomodoro Technique, designed to increase productivity. The concept is to work for 25 minutes, then take a five-minute break. Then, after three cycles, take a longer break.

When possible, I try to switch activities entirely after 20 minutes. If this is not possible and I can see a portion of my students drifting, then I will play something on the screen for us to watch. For example, at the younger levels, we might complete a dance video on YouTube. In the older grades, I might show "People are Awesome Clean" on YouTube, or we would do a quick "Would you rather." If it is at the start of the year, I will share one or two of their growth projects (explained in the next chapter). I might also share one of their Flipgrids. It truly depends on the day.

The point is to create a pattern, so your students know a break is coming. As a result, the class no longer becomes 60 or 90 minutes of listening, note-taking, and practice. Instead, they understand that a change and brain reset will be in about 20 minutes, so they can push through distraction and stay on task.

Limiting Access to Cell Phones This is another section you will need to decide what works for you. It might also be necessary to get the support of your admin. What follows is what works for me.

I do not allow students to use cell phones or sit near their phones during the first and last month of each semester. Instead, students must place their phones deep into their bags, and then their bags go into a designated space in the room. Then, during the last two minutes of class, everyone gets their bags and ensures they have their phones.

There is some resistance for the first few days; however, this is also the time we talk about growth mindset, technology, goal-setting, and perseverance. For almost all students, there is an acceptance of the cell phone procedures.

How do I address the students who don't comply? I extend the no-phone policy for ALL students and keep track of it on the board. Eventually, there is compliance. I will also speak to the student individually, and if it is a repeated problem, I will call home. I will rarely include administration for non-compliance on issues that are not safety risks as I believe it will break trust.

Further, after the first week, I build trust with my students by doing Blookets and Kahoots as the last activity of the class. If all students participate, then we keep doing the activity. If a few students are non-compliant, then I speak with them separately. Finally, if there is a larger group of non-compliance, we stop the activities until we reestablish trust.

I realize this may be drastic; however, I learned that students generally comply with proper structure and explanation. Remember, most students desire to feel success. Therefore, when they know that overuse of technology can inhibit their success, there tends to be much less resistance.

In closing, the suggestions above are just suggestions. They may fit into your teaching style, or they may not work for you. For example, if classroom management is a struggle for your classroom, then flexible seating might be something you wait on until your students embrace a growth mindset.

> **Growth Mindset**
>
> Growth mindset helped me alot this semester. When I first came to this class we started with growth mindset. This helped me reach my inner thought of what I am really capable of. Growth Mindset helps me in school and outside of school. I think I will really use this as I proceed through highschool. The group activities and other growth mindset assignments is something new to me. None of my teachers ever introduced this to me. It helps my study and organizational skills. I recommend that every 8th grader coming to high school next year use this valuable technique because it would really be useful.

> Personally, having a growth mindset has opened my eyes to certain things. For example, have you noticed how many students preform around the same in most classes? This could be because they have given up or accepted the fact that "This is the best I can do." If these same students would decide to not accept how their doing and attempt to be even better. They can achieve much more. Thank you Dr. Enrig for introducing the Growth Mindset to us!

Notes and Doodles

Chapter 5
Growth Activities

The following is a collection of activities that are helpful for me in developing growth-focused students. Depending on the level of my students, I will adapt them year over year or omit ones that are not appropriate.

The First Days

During the first 2-3 days of school, I will focus on developing a growth mindset, technology use, and perseverance. If there is a mandated PreTest, then that will take precedence. Here are slides from 2018. The Google Slideshow is available at bit.ly/lgf118.

Essential Questions & Success Criteria

- How do the expectations for the classroom contribute to my success?
  - I can set myself up for a semester of success
- What is the growth mindset and how can I implement it into my life?
  - I can describe the growth mindset.
  - I can list at least three ways I can incorporate a growth mindset in my life.

Agenda - Part One

- Welcome Back & Lesson Overview
- Expectations
- Reflections
- Excerpts from Previous Students

Expectations

- Arrive on time to learn
- Settle quickly - hoods and hats off
- Utilize technology effectively
- Remain focused on the task at hand
- Communicate appropriately -
  Whole group, small group, individual

One of my frequent sayings is "Research says..." and then I share the research; this is vital because I believe students are more likely to comply when they understand the "why." At the high school level, we watch Dweck's Power of Yet; at younger grades, I will find another video.

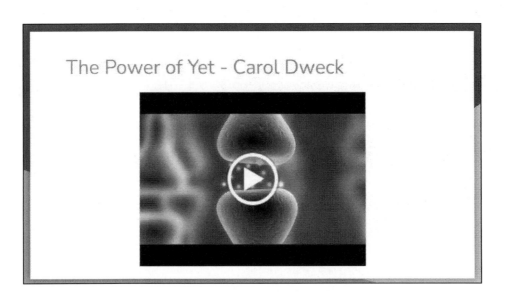

The Power of Yet - Carol Dweck

> ### 9th grade Algebra Student
>
> A growth mindset is having positivity throughout life. You must make mistakes and learn from them to improve on yourself to be a better person. Life isn't always perfect, we all have breaking points and times when we're stuck. We struggle, but that's when we have to pick ourselves up and think, "I have fallen, what shall I do to pick myself up." That's when options pour in like a waterfall and you pick the one that's best for you. You make that change in your life and begin a new and better chapter.

Who is it?

After sharing the foundation of a growth mindset, we start looking at other people who changed their lives by implementing a growth mindset (even if the person didn't know they were doing it). The presentations are from former students, and you are welcome to use them in your class. This assignment becomes their first task; as it is unrelated to the standards, I do not put it in the gradebook. Eventually, most students will complete the task as they like their work displayed to their peers.

The assignment is to create a five-slide presentation in the following format:

    Slide 1: History of the person (no names)
    Slide 2: Turning Point
    Slide 3: Road to Greatness
    Slide 4: Now...
    Slide 5: Reveal the person

They need to keep their selection a secret. Then, when we use the project as a brain break, I display their work, and as people think they know the growth-minded individual, they will raise their hands. After Slide 4, everyone shares who they believe it is, then we do the reveal. Here are some samples:

History

- **His father lost his job when he was young**
- **He lost his home at a young age**
- **Help work in a factory to keep living at age 14**
- **He started to explore his comedic talents in his teen life**
- **At age 15 he made his first appearance as a comedian but ended badly**

Turning Point

- His perseverance led him to regularly appear in the Toronto comedy club
- Dropped out of high school to become a full-time comedian

Road to Greatness

- Continued to work on comedic talents and appeared in some films

Now...

- Has won 4 Golden Globe Awards and 6 nominations
- Has won 5 MTV awards

Bibliography

http://www.jimcarreyonline.com/info/biography_full.html

https://sgargabonzi.files.wordpress.com/2012/06/jim-carrey.jpg

http://www.lifetimetv.co.uk/biography/biography-jim-carrey

History

- Grew up in a three-bedroom bungalow home in Barbados with many brothers and sisters
- Was deeply affected by father's addiction to crack cocaine and alcohol
- Suffered excruciating headaches almost everyday
- Parents divorced

Turning Point

- Health began to improve
- Took an interest in singing
- Formed a musical trio with two of her classmates and got discovered by American producer Evan Rogers
- Sent demo tracks to different record labels

Road to Greatness

- Got signed to Def Jam Recordings by Jay-Z in 2005
- Debut single charted top five on the charts in fifteen countries, including at number two on the U.S Billboard Hot 100 and the U.K Singles Chart
- Debut album charted top ten on the Billboard 200 and received a gold certification from the RIAA
- Sold over two million copies

Her "Now" is a bit old:

Now...

- Has a net worth of $230 million
- Has earned 125 awards including 8 Grammys, from 411 nominations
- Recent album was certified double platinum

This project is special because as we progress through their presentations, we learn about each other while learning about a growth mindset. In addition, most students pick a person they already admire, so they also realize that everyone overcomes challenges.

Learning Styles

During my undergraduate degree in 1999, an adjunct professor did the following lesson with us. The activity was so eye-opening that I use it every year. You can access the slides at bit.ly/lgf218.

First, I give my students an index card and ask them to do the following:

Index Card Set-up - Lined Side

Name	Period:

Power of Growth Mindset
1)
2)

Kid President
1)
2)

Index Card Set-up - Blank Side

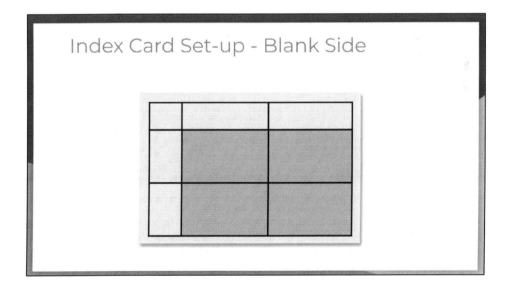

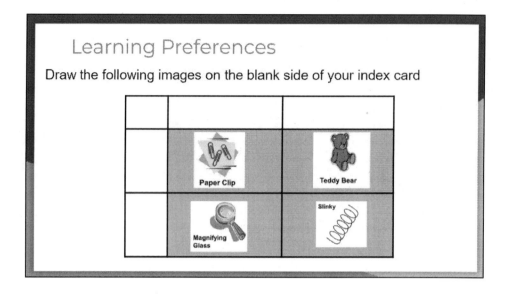

Then I use the following script:

When looking at the four objects, you will pick the one that shares the same qualities with you.

For example, a paper clip helps with organization. A teddy bear is used for comfort and can be a friend. A magnifying glass looks at things deeply, and a slinky can be all over the place. Okay, think about the object while I tell you how each object likes to learn. You will then decide which object most reflects how you learn.

 A paper clip student wants me to say: Okay, class, today we will learn about frogs. First, read Chapter 5; then complete questions 1-10. Paper clip students like to know precisely what they need to do so they can just get to work.

 A teddy bear student wants me to say: Okay, class, today we will learn about frogs. First, get yourself into groups. You can work with anyone you want. Then, go through Chapter 5 together. Talk about any topic you are confused by; each of you will need to turn in answers to questions 1-10. Teddy bear students do best when they can work with others. It is easier for them to learn when they can talk a topic through.

 A magnifying glass student wants to hear the following: Okay, class, today we will learn about frogs. First, go to Chapter 5, and read the objectives. Then, skim over the chapter and find one area that is interesting to you. Then, you have permission to use your device to research that concept more deeply. After, I expect you to share what you learned with everyone.

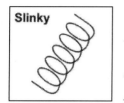

A slinky student wants to hear the following: Okay, class, today we will learn about frogs. First, go to Chapter 5, and read the objectives. Then, skim over the chapter and look at the questions. Your task is to create anything you want to show me that you have mastered the objectives. Want to write a song? Great! Make a poster? Sure! Create a slideshow? No problem. Whatever you want to make to show me that you have learned the objectives works for me.

Now, thinking about what I described, circle the object you most identify with. If you must circle two objects, you can put a number 1 next to the one you are strongest in.

Everyone circled their choice? Let me explain what this means, and yes, I share all of this with my learners:

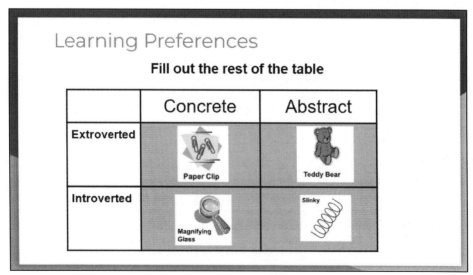

Extroverted Paper clips and teddy bears tend to be extroverted learners. Extroverted learners learn best from getting information from outside sources. It might be a teacher-given resource, like a book, or it might be from discussing the topic with other people.

Introverted Magnifying glass and slinky students tend to be introverted learners. Introverted learners learn best when they can make their own meaning from the topic. They might be annoyed if they are thinking about a concept and people keep talking and sharing their own ideas. This makes it challenging because introverted students need time to process. They may like music or complete silence; however, they usually need time to do their own thinking.

Concrete Paper clips and magnifying glasses are concrete learners. They tend to like facts and patterns. Math might be easier for them because it is routine, but it is not always the case. They thrive when they know what to expect.

Abstract Teddy bear and slinky students are abstract learners. So they might hate it if the teacher stood at the board and gave notes daily; being asked to read a chapter and answer questions is dreadful. They want to be creative or at least talk.

The lesson continues:

> Now, think of a teacher you enjoyed. How did they act? Were they paper clip teachers who gave you notes and told you precisely what you needed to know? Were they teddy bear teachers? Did they love to talk, tell stories, and let you work in groups? Were they magnifying glass teachers, always explaining why something happened? Or were they slinky teachers, just super creative and a bit disorganized?
>
> Were your favorite teachers most like you?
>
> Okay, raise your hand if you are a paper clip? Teddy bear? Magnifying glass? Slinky? Wow, look at the variety.
>
> As I plan my lessons, I strive to have activities that match your learning preference during each class. For example, sometimes you have to answer specific questions, and other times you get to be more social. Next to each activity, I will include pictures of which learning preference the task aligns with so you know what to expect and that your turn is coming.
>
> Please, respect your peers. If you are a paper clip or teddy bear, and we are doing activities to help our magnifying glasses and slinky students, please be quiet and give them the space to think and process.

Don't shut down if you are magnifying glass or slinky when I assign you to a group to work on a concept. Instead, use this as a growth moment, and share your thoughts with your group.

If you are a teddy bear or slinky, please take notes from the board. I know it can be annoying; just do it. I promise what I share will matter. If you are a paper clip or magnifying glass, and I ask you to do an assignment that requires you to be creative and think differently, recognize that you will still likely learn something and that you have creativity in you.

You must understand that our goal is for all of us to pass this class. Not simply pass this class, but master the content with scores higher than 85%. You are individual students working together so that all of us can grow.

After the lesson, I collect the cards to review and sort the index cards during planning. Then, on my attendance sheet, I note their object selection next to each student's name. Further, I tally how many paper clip, teddy bear, magnifying glass, and slinky students are in each class.

It will be very tempting to create activities that align with your style of learning. However, I encourage you to grow just a bit and recognize that students in your classroom learn differently than you do. As a result, you will see a change in your classroom.

The use of the four objects to determine learning preference differs from the verbal, auditory, and kinesthetic frameworks we might strive to address. Yet, the Learning Style strategy shared above has been way more informative for me. It is quick, does not require multiple questionnaires, and is accurate enough to give me a snapshot of who is in my room.

Do I have predominantly paperclips and magnifying glasses? Then we do a proportionally higher amount of note-taking. Do I have a class full of teddy bears? Then there are more opportunities for turn and talks. Do I have a group of magnifying glasses? Then I ensure there are quiet moments so they can work. Lots of slinkys? I might let them lead the brain breaks or adapt an assignment based on their interests.

There are still opportunities to honor each learning style in a virtual environment—Google Slides, Microsoft PowerPoint, or even Classkick work great for group work. In addition, students can be provided creative projects, like Flipgrids. Later in the chapter, I will share my favorite growth mindset assignment, which is only four words long and can be done virtually.

Student Teachers

Some of my favorite lessons are when I do not teach, and my students become the "expert" in the content. Essentially, I write every topic in the unit (or semester) on the board. Students then choose their topic and if they want to work individually, in pairs, or larger groups. Good teaching would suggest that I include a rubric for grading; as this task is not graded, I don't.

Doesn't this mean the students won't complete the assignment because there is no grade? Please, do not underestimate the value of collective responsibility. If a student does not complete the task, the entire class will suffer. When you continue to encourage your students and have high expectations, they will rise to the task. Further, you likely know which students might not do this well, so meet with them immediately after it is assigned. Remind them that they are capable and their peers are counting on them. Give them some support with where they need to look to find the information. (Think of Vygotsky's Zone of Proximal Development.) Eventually, they will complete the assignment, even though no grade is attached.

I give more structure for the first assignment: typically asking all students to review the topic, address any misconceptions, and provide practice questions. Next, the students get to work. In a virtual environment, I suggest all students create a few slides on their topic. Then, I combine the slides into one review file. Finally, the day before the "practice test," students take over the classroom. They cover the topic, share what to look out for, and provide practice questions for those interested.

Over the years, student teachers have helped my advanced students think differently about the content, and my below-level students feel confident about at least one test standard. Once they feel comfortable in one area, it is easier to ask them to pick the next topic to master. Eventually, they make it through all the necessary topics for the unit, and we celebrate each success.

Data Trackers

At the earlier grade levels, goal sheets and data trackers help develop growth-focused students. In addition, data trackers are beneficial if you implement programs to close gaps. The following are actual trackers from previous students, though the photographs are stock pictures. Student photos are vital if your classroom involves consultant teachers, ESOL, special education services, or volunteers.

The top portion of the page includes questions about the future. I strive to help students see how every task, no matter how mundane, could potentially help them reach their goals; I speak about these conversations in Chapter

7: The Extras. The reverse side of the Data Tracker includes spaces for them to set goals for future dates.

When I am an adult, I want to be a(n) Preschool teacher, or a writer.

What I love most about middle school is: There are new classes, and new lunch choices.

Next year, I am excited about 7th grade.

Next year, I am concerned about C- d- B- (low grades)

If I could go anywhere in the world, I would go Disney World or Australia.

MobyMax

	Date	Grade Equivalent	Effort
1		2.2	
2			
3			
4			
5			

My goal for the next time I complete the MobyMax Placement Test is to be at GE 2.5. To achieve this goal, I will _____

The areas I still need help with are percents, fractions, and multiplying fractions.

When I am an adult, I want to be a(n) __Teacher__

What I love most about middle school is: __Art Class__

Next year, I am excited about __Art Class__

Next year, I am concerned about __all of the hard things in school that I have troble with. And Grades.__

If I could go anywhere in the world, I would go __North Carolina, Cape Cod, Disney World, hawii, Beach and Pool.__

MobyMax

	Date	Grade Equivalent	Effort
1		4.2	
2			
3			
4			
5			

My goal for the next time I complete the MobyMax Placement Test is to be at GE __4.6__. To achieve this goal, I will __practice more.__

The areas I still need help with are __all of it but not division, multiplication, adding and subtracting.__

Growth Mindset: Slinky Assignment

If you teach a full-year course, this next assignment may be helpful after returning from winter break. The first two days back, I give my students my favorite task:

Growth Mindset: Slinky Assignment

For the most part, I do not provide any other guidance than those four words. Again, not great teaching in terms of the lack of rubric; however, as it is not graded, I don't mind. Also, there will be some paper clips and magnifying glasses, which may need some further hints or suggestions. Typically, most students do well and appreciate the freedom.

Over the years, I received many unique projects that I would never have considered. For example, some students create a traditional PowerPoint, while others may make a poster. In addition, I've received podcasts, PowToon cartoons, and even a dance.

Unlike the Who is it? assignment explained earlier in the chapter where I anonymously used their presentations of growth-focused individuals, the sharing of the Growth Mindset: Slinky Assignment with the class is entirely optional.

Student Reflections

My final suggestion for growth activities is to offer students time to reflect on the process. At the end of every unit, I schedule a 10-minute free-write, and yes, in Math. Students reflect on growth mindset, and once they finish, they can write anything they want. They also know that I want it to be honest. So, if they think learning about growth mindset is a waste of time, let me know. I will still have them go through the lessons, but at least I know. After, I read every response and write reflections back. The students then get their papers back to track their thoughts about the growth-focused lessons over the year.

Typed Student Reflection from the Next Page:

The growth mindset impacts scores in math by helping me believe I actually can do it. When I see something I don't know how to do I automatically didn't do it and just skipped it without trying which is called fixed mindset. But now I attempt new things even if I didn't learn it or its challenging which is called growth mindset. As in instead of going around problems I go through them and TRY to conquer them. My scores have shifted and increased so much. I thought I would always be bad at math but now... I'm actually not that bad. If I had a fixed mindset I would be in the same place or worse, below that. Now I have hope and a B in math.

Dr. Michelle Ihrig

1) 80%

2) The growth mindset impacts my scores in math by helping me believe I actually can do it. When I see something I don't know how to do I automatically didn't do it and just skipped it without trying, which is called fixed mindset. But now I attempt new things even if I didn't learn it or it's challenging, which is called growth mindset. As in instead of going around my problems, I go through them and TRY to conquer them. My scores have shifted and increased so much. I thought I would always be bad at math but now... I'm actually not that bad. If I had a fixed mindset I would be in the same place or worse, below that. Now I have hope and a B in math.

woohoo!
True!

Daijah- you are one of the people who has truly grown in the growth mindset AND in math. I am so, so, so, so PROUD of you! When you try and you succeed, you light up the whole room and convince others to try without even knowing it! So thank you, thank you!
Dr. mi.

In closing, embedding aspects of growth mindset into your classroom does not need to consume a significant amount of time. Granted, in the first days, you may feel "behind;" however, plan for it. Then, with your content team/PLC, build in those days… or if you are flying solo, build backward from the test days.

My students learn that when we are together, our time matters. Whether it is learning our curriculum, reviewing data, or taking tests, even the unmotivated can be motivated because it's not a class just of traditional content. The five-minute growth-focused activity may just be enough to help them stay invested.

Remember, none of this started as a way to help students excel in life. I taught them about growth mindset because I wanted their math scores to increase. They took the concept and applied it to their lives.

> In Dr. Ihrig class we focus on growth mindset. We've done activities like posters, writing about it and watching videos. Was it worth learning about it in the end? Yes, I think it was worth it. It gave me a healthier and better mindset than with the one I started with. Having a healthy mindset is important to have in the future, when in a heavy competive enviroment. Having a growing mindset helps you learn faster, which is very helpful in a fast pace job. Growth Mindset is a more healthy and is a better mindset for learning.

In Dr. Ihrig's class this year growth mindset was a big topic that stayed the same throughout the year. It actually helped me with my goals not only in this class but in other classes as well. I came into this year motivated, scared, but ready. Then in the middle of the school year, I was so over it. I truly believe with out you and growth mindset in my ear I would have been like fudge it.

- growth mindset
  - better grades
  - specific goals
- complete goals
- relationships better
- I'm more open
- I'm basically a sofmore

This lesson will be with me until I'm done with school.

Notes and Doodles

Chapter 6

Communication

One group who may struggle with the idea of spending class time teaching students about growth mindset instead of the curriculum could be families. Their confusion or concern could become highly evident if you do not share your philosophy at the start of the school year. The following practices typically satisfy 80% of families from Day 1. After the second unit test, about 90% of families are on board. Eventually, most will get there, especially when they see the growth in their child.

Welcome Letter and Video

The Welcome Letter is your first chance to share the concept of a growth mindset. My letters are relatively basic; however, my welcome video is critical. Here is a link to my welcome video from 2021: bit.ly/docintro21. I gear the video to the students and send it to students and parents. I could spend the following pages writing the key topics; however, everything you need is in the video above.

Overshare

I love technology. Our district uses a platform called Synergy for attendance and some forms of communication. There is a wonderful feature that will allow me to email all my families, a few families, or just a single family. I can also include students. As I shared briefly in the Logistics chapter, I grade daily. It makes it easier for me to stay on top of each formative assignment and gives parents and students a clear understanding of current levels of mastery.

At the beginning of the school year, I will email students and parents the titles of any missing assignments. The task takes me about 10 minutes, and work completion increases drastically after the first weeks. Then, I encourage students and parents to monitor mastery and work completion through weekly progress reports, discussed later.

The following is an actual email sent to selected students and parents. You will notice the reference to a form. With all the make-ups I allow students to complete, I used to have students complete a form. However, I discovered that I prefer them to email me allowing me to give them a quick response back so they know I made the update.

> **Michelle Ihrig**
> To:
> Mon 10/11/2021 2:04 PM
>
> 1a
>
> Good afternoon students.
>
> This is Dr. Ihrig from 3rd period math. I am writing about the <u>Unit 1b Presentation on Flipgrid.</u>
>
> <u>The topic was decimal operations.</u>
>
> **<u>You are receiving this email because you did not complete this assignment, which is a TEST grade.</u>**
>
> **You will have until 7am Tomorrow morning to address this assignment or the grade stands.**
>
> **Please go to the class board to get the links. Please watch the videos on the Announcement tab to see high quality examples.**
>
> Once you finish, please complete the form located on the class board from last week. I will only grade assignments listed on that form.
>
> Thank you,
>
> Dr. Ihrig

I will also send emails to students and families that include any opportunities for make-up work. Here are some examples:

Dear Parent/Guardian,

*** is in danger of failing Algebra I for the first quarter. There are * missing homework assignments which are significantly impacting the grade.

But there is still time to raise the grade!

For every 30 minutes of time your child spends on Khan Academy, they will be able replace one of the missing homework assignments with a 100%. This will significantly increase their score. Students access Khan Academy through their Google Classroom. There is a link for them to follow to the specific work, and students should complete the practice problems, watching videos as needed.

Students are allowed to raise their grade in Algebra because our class philosophy is We Grow/ Nosotros Crecemos…. In essence, learning is about the journey. Students learn the value of a growth mindset and how with effort, they can achieve success. Hopefully, such mindsets will transfer to other classes and other areas of life.

Please contact me with any questions.

Warmly,

Michelle Ihrig

From: Michelle Ihrig
Sent: Wednesday, December 15, 2021 4:07 PM
To:
Subject: email;

Dear 7th grade Students and Families,

The gradebook is now fully updated as of Noon today. If you emailed me if your child completed an assignment, please check ParentVue or look for the progress report coming in moments.

Please note:

1. I will NO longer accept edPuzzles. With so many, the impact on the grade is very small. If I mistyped an edPuzzle grade, <u>the student</u> can email me.
2. I will only accept the following assignments until Wednesday, December 15, <u>at 8:00am</u> because these assignments have the MOST impact on the overall grade.
    1. Summative Category: Any test with a 0 from ___ *Assess* can be completed
    2. Summative Category: Any *Classkick Performance Task* – Note, this **self-grades** so students can get 100s and it is a TEST GRADE (just make sure to show work)!!
        1. 1c Performance Task
        2. 2a Performance Task
        3. 2b Performance Task
        4. 3a Performance Task (New assignment completed in class on Tuesday 12/14)
    3. Presentation Category (Counts as Test): Flipgrid Presentation
        1. 1c Flipgrid: https://flipgrid.com.
        2. 2a Flipgrid: https://flipgrid.com/75...
        3. 2b Flipgrid: https://flipgrid.com/89...
        4. 2c Flipgrid: https://flipgrid.com/b3...
3. The 7.2c Inequalities Test was from today. Students will take a similar test on Wednesday which can increase their grade if they perform better on that test. The test on Wednesday will not decrease their grade any further.

Students MUST complete the form in My Digital Sessions if they want their tests, performance tasks, or presentations graded.

Thank you,
Dr. Michelle Ihrig

Proper Emails

This next suggestion is something I am a bit of a stickler on, and it also may take some families a while to get used to it. Regarding communication, especially about grades, I require that my students be the primary point of contact, and all communication must be done in a very specific way. In a face-to-face environment, this may not be necessary; however, I still believe proper digital communication is a valuable skill for life.

How to Email Dr. Ihrig

1: You must use your SCHOOL email :)
If you do not, then I will email you back and ask you to do so before I respond to your question.

2: Be specific: The more details the better
I have a question about my grade for Adding Integers on 8/15/2021. - No date, no response, if your question is about grades. If it is about attendance, be specific about which days you are concerned about.

3: Include your full name and class period
Somewhere mention your name and your class period. It makes it easier for me to look things up for you.

The first email for any new topic
should be formal and provide details:
Dear Dr. Ihrig, this is .... in period ... writing about...

After, we will write back and forth more casually.

First, I share my expectations with my students on the first day (see image). Then, I send the image to students and parents to reiterate my expectations. Finally, I post it to our online classroom. When students email me, I expect them to follow these guidelines. If they don't, I simply email them back and ask them to try again. I may also include the guidelines, just in case.

> **From:** Michelle Ihrig
> **Sent:** Friday, March 11, 2022 2:48 PM
> **To:**
> **Subject:** RE: 0447 - Math 6 Q3 - Math Class Today
>
> I graded the one from today. Are there other ones you did?
> As a reminder, please <u>include the names of the assignments</u>
>
> ---
>
> **From:**
> **Sent:** Friday, March 11, 2022 2:37 PM
> **To:** Michelle Ihrig
> **Subject:** RE: 0447 - Math 6 Q3 - Math Class Today
>
> Hello its   form 1st period im done with the flipgrid presentation

The sixth grade is the youngest grade I implemented email procedures. When parents email me about grades, I will refer them to the grading portal for information. If they email me about a specific assignment, I kindly remind the parents that I only adjust grades based on student emails and ask them to prompt their child.

Regarding any topic OTHER than updating an assignment, I strive to answer the email within one day. Emails that need me to review an assignment and update the gradebook are flagged in Outlook and typically only updated on Thursdays.

To show you what students are capable of, the following are some emails from my students, and there are hundreds of other examples I could share.

From: Michelle Ihrig
Sent: Thursday, March 31, 2022 10:23 AM
To:

Subject: RE: 0658 - Math 6 Q4 - Math This Week

All set 😊

From:

Sent: Monday, March 28, 2022 6:28 PM
To: Michelle Ihrig
Subject: Re: 0658 - Math 6 Q4 - Math This Week

My name is   and I am in your 1st period math class and:
I forgot to email you this morning, and right now I was reviewing some work and I wanted to let you know if you could check my 6.U7.Coordinate Plane (3/28/2022) slide 4 please.
Thanks,
Nahomy

From: Michelle Ihrig
Sent: Wednesday, November 10, 2021 12:00 PM
To:
Subject: RE: Power outage

Great email!
Thanks, and okay 😊

From: Mason
Sent:
To: Michelle Ihrig
Subject: Power outage

Dear Ms.Ihrig 7th grade 5th period Mason
There has been a power outage so I might be late for class
Mason

From: Michelle Ihrig
Sent: Wednesday, October 20, 2021 8:19 AM
To:
Subject: RE: Grades.

Hi Khloe, good email. You can redo any task except for the interim. 😊

From: Khloe
Sent: Tuesday, October 19, 2021 4:26 PM
To: Michelle Ihrig
Subject: Grades.

Hi Dr. Ihrig, this is Khloe   in 1st period. I saw my grades and i have two 50's i want to know how i can make my grade up so i have good ones, im willing to do any task, thank you some much Khloe

Our kids are capable of so much. Picture these middle school students when they need to email a possible college or employer in a couple of years. We need to set high expectations for them. They will rise to the challenge.

Finally, you may have a few parents push back on enforcing the student-as-the-point-of-contact expectation. Just remind them that your goal is to help their child excel in life with a growth mindset. Reassure them that if any serious situation occurs, you will be in contact... and if you follow the communication model I am sharing, they will believe you!

Weekly Progress Reports

Earlier in this chapter, I wrote about oversharing. Sending weekly progress reports to students and families is one way that I overshare. Because I grade first attempts of formative assignments daily and designate Thursdays for any resubmitted assignments, my gradebook is complete every Friday. Of course, there are some exceptions; for example, more rigorous projects will take me longer to grade.

| Class Name: (Q3) Ihrig, M Math 7 Q3(5) SEC:0452 |
| Grading Period: Quarter 3 |

Here are the grades as of 3pm. STUDENTS - If I missed something, please email me. I will fix it the next school day. So far, I've graded over 5000 assignments... I make mistakes. Let me know, and we can adjust it. The LAST DAY I will accept missing work will be Monday, March 14. This will give me time to update missing assignments and time for students to make sure the grades are correct. Thank you for working so hard and being your very best! Dr. Ihrig

Area			Mark	Comment	% of Grade	Notes
Overall Class Grade		88.5%	89			
Formative (40.00%)		91.7%	92		40.0%	
Summative (50.00%)		85.7%	86		50.0%	
Presentation (10.00%)		90.0%	90		10.0%	
Assignments						
Flipgrid: Me in 60 seconds (Presentation)	1/11/2022	100.0%	100		5.0%	
EdP:Unit Rates (Formative)	1/12/2022	87.0%	87		2.7%	
EdP: Percent Decimal Fractions (Formative)	1/13/2022	75.6%	75.63		2.7%	
CK: Percent Overview (Formative)	1/18/2022	98.0%	98		2.7%	
EdP: Percent of a Number (Formative)	1/20/2022	94.0%	94		2.7%	
CK: Percent Of is (Formative)	1/20/2022	100.0%	100		2.7%	
EdP: Proportional Relationships (Formative)	1/24/2022	90.4%	90.4		2.7%	

The above progress report is a sampling of what I send out. First is a message, always written to students. In addition, I provide a timeframe for when I completed the grades and any other relevant information.

If you notice the assignments, the pattern is consistent. EdP stands for EdPuzzles and CK is for Classkick. In addition, you can see that I don't use any other naming conventions other than the name of the skill the student is attempting to master.

Further, notice how some of the assignments include decimals. For example, the EdP Percent Decimal Fractions task scored 75.63. This means the student's first attempt earned a 63%. The student then resubmitted the assignment and achieved a 75%.

For the EdP: Proportional Relationships, the score is 90.4. As there is only one digit after the decimal, the original score was 40%. The resubmitted score was 90%. Therefore, the student's mastery of proportional relationships rose from 40% to 90% on this task. Note: I need to shout out Mr. M, who taught me the decimal trick for retakes.

One more note about using decimals for retakes: it is a source of data when you have conversations with families about grades. In one glance, I can immediately inform the parent how many assignments the child attempted again.

Class Name: (Q4) Ihrig, M Math 6 Q4(1) SEC:0658
Grading Period: Quarter 4

Hello Students and Families! Here are the updated grades. All assignments were due YESTERDAY. Students can have until this FRIDAY to complete missing work and earn passing grades. No new work will be added, so this represents the final grades, unless the student completes make-up work or extra credit. Thanks! Dr. Ihrig

Area			Mark	Comment	Notes
Overall Class Grade		61.8%	62	5 Missing	
Assignments					
EdP: Dot Plots and Data (Formative)	3/17/2022	70.6%	70.56		
EdP: Histograms (Formative)	3/17/2022	70.6%	70.56		
CK: Measures of Center (Formative)	3/18/2022	85.6%	85.64		
CK.Data.Performance Task (Summative)	3/21/2022	72.0%	72		
6.U6.Test (Summative)	3/22/2022	70.4%	70.43		
CK: 6.U7.Rational Numbers, Absolute Values, Number Line (03/24/2022) (Formative)	3/24/2022	100.0%	100		
EdP: Coordinate Plane (Formative)	3/25/2022	60.1%	60.12		
CK: Coordinate Plane (Formative)	3/28/2022	12.0%	12		
CTLS Unit 7 Test (Summative)	3/29/2022	25.0%	25		

Let's look at the previous student's progress report as an example. This student redid five of the lowest assignments. Unfortunately, the student did not take advantage of redoing the CK: Coordinate Plane assignment or the Summative Test. Because there are no decimals in the grades, I can easily communicate the information with the family.

Because this student's overall score is a 62%, it warranted a quick follow-up phone call home to explain how proud I am that the student focused on retakes and to guide the family on which assignments need a revisit. Further, the computer program my district uses also allows us to track missing assignments, so I can direct the family to those assignments (which are hidden from this picture).

A helpful hint: be consistent. If you tell your families that you will send progress reports weekly, do so. For example, I send my progress reports on Fridays so students can catch up on the weekend.

Now, there are times when I can't meet my deadline. So, what do I do? First, I let my families know. For example, my students were sometimes so outstanding at resubmitting assignments that I could not regrade everything by my deadline. For instance, I had over 60 assignments to regrade in one week. So, I send the progress reports out anyway with a note at the top that I am still working on resubmissions; however, the other grades for the week are accurate. Then, I provide a timeframe and stick to it – usually the following Monday. My students and families are still aware of any new missing assignments. Also, the only change in the grade from Friday to Monday will be an increase based on resubmitted work.

A final thought about progress reports is that some people may think they are unnecessary, given that, depending on the district, the family can access the same information online. I have discovered this: if you can easily send the reports, please do them. If your school's grading system cannot send progress reports, it is understandable to skip this step. Otherwise, please try…here's why:

Our lives are busy. Because of my district's robust software, it takes me less than 10 minutes to send progress reports to 150 students and families. Accessing the parent portal and seeing grades can take five to ten minutes for a family. Five minutes multiplied by 150 families amounts to 750 minutes or 12.5 hours. If we include the students checking their portal for missed work, students and families could collectively spend 25 hours a week reviewing the status of their grades in my class…. OR I could take 10 minutes of my time and send them an informative, computer-generated email to a source they check daily.

    Some of my colleagues choose to invest their time in creative lesson planning. I prefer to focus on consistency in expectations and a heightened level of communication. I am not saying my way is the best. I am simply saying that using a portion of my daily planning period for grading and sending communication moves my students further towards (and beyond) the 85% mastery level than when my lessons were more interest-based and graded on completion. Remember, engaging lessons at low DOK levels will not move students to mastery. However, students will rise to the challenge and meet high expectations if we invest the time in creating enough opportunities for them.

Dr. Michelle Ihrig

"I believe growth mindset was a good use of my time. I may not use growth mindset in math, however, I use it plenty of times in my every day life. Growth mindset helps me accomplish goals more difficult in my mind. The whole purpose was for us to use it for a geometry pretest. However, it has since grown into something bigger than that. I use it for sports, video games, relationships, and getting done my everday activities. Growth mindset can really improve someone's mindset to always wanting to improve on something. Even when I recieve bad grades on tests or assignments, I am able to use growth mindset to help me move on in a positive direction. In summary, growth mindset has been a very big part of my life in ninth grade. It has helped me overcome many things other than school. I am happy to be able to use such a great trait for my future life.

Notes and Doodles

Chapter 7
The Extras

This chapter includes additional thoughts about creating growth-focused classrooms that I could not find a perfect place to share in the other chapters. So, if it seems a bit hodge-podge, it is!

Administration

If you are reading this book, you likely fall into one of two camps: your school leadership decided to implement growth-focused procedures, or this is your idea. I am sure there is some middle ground, and this section targets educators who want to implement growth-focused techniques in their classes, and the administration knows little about the topic.

First, the good news is that you should be able to use several activities without too much administration involvement. In my experience, few school policies would prohibit you from determining your students' learning styles, helping them set goals, or becoming student teachers/leaders in the classroom. So, if you feel that there may be some resistance, at a minimum, you will see success just by implementing those activities in your classroom. Still, if you are concerned, please talk with your admin team.

Next, the grading policies, especially where students can have multiple opportunities to demonstrate mastery, could require administrative approval. If there are five teachers on your collaborative team, and you are the only one which allows students multiple attempts, it could appear to be an unfair advantage. I recommend presenting the idea to your collaborative team first. There may be some opposition; however, an excellent collaborative team collaborates. You have several pages to share from my experience and actual student thoughts about the process.

Perhaps a good first step would be to select an upcoming unit as a team pilot. Then the entire team could implement the procedures, send a note to parents about the strategy, and collect data on the program's success. Then at a subsequent collaborative team meeting, the team could review the data compared to other unit tests and determine if this strategy would make sense moving forward. If your team favors the pilot, please loop in your administrator before starting if they are not already members of your collaborative team.

Most educators would accept the idea of two tests. The only modification you might need is to not include the "practice test" score in the gradebook. Instead, administer the test and provide all the recommended supports;

however, leave it as it is... a practice test with no impact on the overall grade.

I would hope that your administrators would see the success of your growth-focused strategies over time and then embrace them at the content, grade, or school levels. The more exposure young people have to these concepts during the day, the more likely it will become a part of who they are so they can excel throughout their lives.

Behavior Issues

In the first chapters, I discussed those "high-flyers" who are button-pushers. Perhaps because I was so close in age to my first students, I rarely will ever send a situation to the administration to handle. I strongly believe in conversation and learning from the experience.

Over the past decade, this idea of teachers managing behaviors before administrator involvement is becoming more prevalent, especially in schools implementing PBIS: Positive Behavior Interventions and Supports. When I worked in younger grades, students who needed a minute could ask to go to the "take a break room." In the older grades, I might ask if the student needed a minute to listen to music or play a game on their phone. After they calmed down, we would address the issue via conversation.

There was even a time when someone stole a student's phone in my high school classroom. The student left it on their desk, and it went missing. My solution, which I am not necessarily recommending, was to let the students know I was highly disappointed. Also, if the phone wasn't found, everyone would have a consequence; namely, the no phone policy would go back into effect.

I then told them I would step into the hallway so that they could figure out where the phone was. After a few minutes of most students complaining about how I would implement the no phone policy again, a student miraculously located the phone. I did not know who took the phone, so I did not write a referral. Instead, I informed all my other classes about what happened and the impending consequences, and no phone went missing again—high expectations and consistency matter.

The Planet Fitness Story

If there is one area I am still growing in regarding growth mindset, it is my health. For over 20 years, I weighed over 285 pounds. During one of my focused periods of getting healthy, the Planet Fitness incident occurred. Coincidentally, it happened during that first year of teaching students about the growth mindset, and I use the true story every time my students take a significant test or when they just need to hear it again.

Here's what happened:

I was living in Connecticut and wanted to get into the pattern of going to the gym before work. So, I drove 15 minutes to Planet Fitness to get to the gym, passing the school I worked at. Then, I would drive home, pass the school again, get ready, and go to work. (Now, I just get ready at the gym, but at that time, I didn't.)

One morning, in the cold winter, I brushed the snow off my car and made the usual trek. While in the 30-minute circuit area, a woman approached me to see if I wanted to be her workout buddy to help keep her accountable for going to the gym and working out. I politely declined, though I mentioned that if she was at the gym at the same time, she could work out next to me.

A few days later, I noticed the woman again at the gym. We said "good morning," and then she got on the treadmill next to me. So far, all of this is fine… but here is what happened next.

Being at least half my size, she set the treadmill at less than 2mph. She then started talking to me as if the two of us were sitting at a table at Starbucks. I was moving much faster, to the point that conversations were difficult. After five minutes of me providing one-word responses, she did not get the cue and kept talking. Ultimately, I finished the workout, then politely left.

Here's the point: sometimes, the most challenging thing in life is just showing up. Both of us woke up before 5am, put on workout clothes, brushed the fresh snow off our cars, navigated through the winding roads of Connecticut, and arrived at the gym before 6am. It would have been so much easier just to sleep that extra hour.

The difference is that once we arrived at the gym, our mindsets were different. I used my time wisely to get healthier and focus on why I went to the gym. Unfortunately, my potential workout buddy chose not to work out at her best level and desired to be distracted in conversation instead.

I remind my students: you already did the challenging part of the day. You chose to wake up, get dressed, and come to school. You are already here and, depending on your age, are required to be here. You lack the freedom to wander the halls, leave campus, or do other things of your choosing without consequence. So, since you are here, you might as well do your best. What else do you have to do?

Yes, you could play pool on your phone, and you can also do that after school. You can scroll through Instagram or watch TikTok, though neither will help you earn your $100,000 yearly salary. You are already here! You already got dressed, got to school, and are sitting in class. Why not care enough about yourself to do your very best?

Similarly, when my students go to sit for the state milestones, SAT, or any other assessment, I tell them something similar:

You must sit in that seat for the next two hours: no cell phone, no walks in the hall, no games when you finish. Since you are already here, just do your best. If you start to lose focus, play a quick tic-tac-toe game with yourself, then get back on track. When you leave, let there be no question that what you just did was your best work. How awful it would be to learn that one more question correct could have been the difference between a B and an A, a D and a C, or even an F and passing. You owe it to yourself to be the best you.

Student Conversations

There will come times when individual student conversations become necessary. They may relate to behavior issues, motivation, or work completion. When time allows, I will set a day for independent work so that I can speak with each child individually, even if only for a minute.

The main focus of any conversation I have with a student is growth and the future. We look at what is to come. If they are younger, it might be what courses they want to take in high school. If they are middle school or high school students, it is almost always about money. I frequently tell my students that I want them to earn $80,000 a year by the time they are 30 and $100,000 a year by the time they are 35.

If I see a cell phone out during instruction, instead of flipping out on them, I will ask... is that video you are watching or game you are playing more important than earning $100,000 a year? Likewise, if the student comes to me with an issue that they are having about a peer relationship, I ask: is that person worth more than earning several million dollars in your lifetime.

I believe that regardless of circumstances, a person who chooses to implement a growth mindset will go farther in life than someone who chooses not to. Will all my students earn those salaries in the future? Perhaps. Yet, I will still do my best to help them to see past their current grade level in school and to look toward the future they want to create for themselves.

Growth Mindset

Growth mindset is about never giving up and pushing untill the end. No matter the struggles and difficulties, growth mindset never gives up, but strives for a much better result each time. Growth mindset is like perseverence and endurance. Even if you don't win the race, you can still finish it. Growth mindset is not about winning, but about knowing that you did your best and tried very hard. And that next time, you may actually win. But at the moment, finishing the race, and keeping your eyes on the goal to practice harder, is growth mindset. With growth mindset, you don't get depressed when you lose, you feel joy that you tried, and hope that you will win the next race. Growth mindset works like hope, it is a mixture of both perseverence and endurance. Growth mindset is also like faith. Faith that you can do it.
Hebrews 10:39 "We are not among those who draw back and perish, but among those who have faith and will possess life."
Phillipians 4:13 "I can do all things through Christ who stengthens me."

Notes and Doodles

Chapter 8
Take Action

At the beginning of this book, I encouraged you to find even a few ideas that may strengthen your teaching practice. If we sat down over coffee or lunch, I am sure you have several ideas that could inspire my teaching practice.

Over the past chapters, we discussed various themes to help your classroom be growth-focused. We began talking about the power of mindset, not our students' mindsets but our own. We focused on how we decide the weather in our classroom and how our actions can have lifelong implications.

In Chapter 2, the focus was on philosophy changes, including grading policies and a focus on mastery. Then, we discussed testing and the need to refrain from testing practices that may lower our content's rigor. In Chapter 4, I shared how I manage the logistics of my classroom, from lighting to seating to eating.

Chapter 5 was a collection of growth activities focused on learning styles and discovering others who lead growth-focused lives. Then we talked about communication and the value of equipping our students with skills that will last them for years. Lastly, I discussed strategies for implementation with the administration and your collaborative team, as well as how to handle behavior issues and have meaningful future-focused conversations with your students.

The following pages will help you focus or adapt a strategy to pilot and implement. Remember, this is not about doing everything at once. Creating growth-focused classrooms is a process. It took me over 20 years working in K-12 public, charter, and international schools to develop into who I am today, and each year, I grow even more.

> I have come to a frightening conclusion.
> I am the decisive element in the classroom.
> It is my personal approach that creates the climate.
> It is my daily mood that makes the weather.
> As a teacher I possess the tremendous power
> to make a child's life miserable or joyous.
> I can be a tool of torture
> or an instrument of inspiration.
> I can humiliate or humor, hurt or heal.
> In all situations it is my response that decides
> whether a crisis will be escalated or de-escalated
> and a student humanized or de-humanized.
> Dr. Haim G. Ginott

Dr. Michelle Ihrig

Area #1 Action Plan

Targeted area & Page #	
Reason for this selection	
What needs to be changed/ added	
What obstacles could occur	
Who needs to be part of the process	
Reflections	

Area #2 Action Plan

Targeted area & Page #	
Reason for this selection	
What needs to be changed/ added	
What obstacles could occur	
Who needs to be part of the process	
Reflections	

Area #3 Action Plan

Targeted area & Page #	
Reason for this selection	
What needs to be changed/ added	
What obstacles could occur	
Who needs to be part of the process	
Reflections	

Area #4 Action Plan

Targeted area & Page #	
Reason for this selection	
What needs to be changed/ added	
What obstacles could occur	
Who needs to be part of the process	
Reflections	

Dr. Michelle Ihrig

Area #5 Action Plan

Targeted area & Page	
Reason for this selection	
What needs to be changed/ added	
What obstacles could occur	
Who needs to be part of the process	
Reflections	

Notes and Doodles

Notes and Doodles

Notes and Doodles

Notes and Doodles

Notes and Doodles

Notes and Doodles

About the Author

Dr. Michelle Ihrig is an author/educator based in Atlanta, Georgia. Her passion is inspiring others. She believes:

When people believe in themselves,
they are unstoppable.
Dreams become obtainable,
Success is fathomable,
and Hope abounds.

Dr. Ihrig is a certified educator in Mathematics, Special Education, English as an Additional Language, Gifted Education, Online Education, and Administration. Her doctoral focus was on best practices of inclusive education at international schools.

Dr. Ihrig is also the author of the
Live Growth Focused series for students and grown-ups,
Scripture Life Devotionals, and
Black Bear Coloring Literacy Books.
All are available on Amazon.

Made in the USA
Columbia, SC
10 October 2022